This workbook is dedicated to all the children that have taught me that self esteem grows if it is carefully nourished, nurtured and promoted.

To my children and husband whom it is a pleasure to love!
To my sister Bachi whom I love so much.

Special thanks to my husband who helped me edit this and read it with me numerous times always patiently!

Thanks to Francisco for his patience and amazing creativity!

Diana Malca Chern.

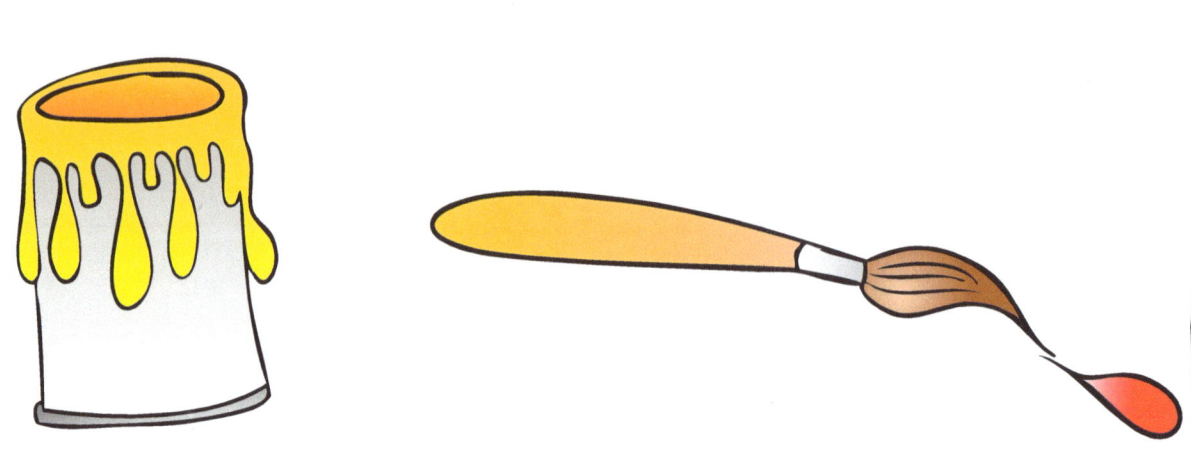

Dear Parents, Educators and Counselors, Thank you for acquiring this wonderful workbook on self esteem enhancement.

This workbook includes one of the most powerful and complete definitions of self esteem.

The "Declaration of Self Esteem" was written by world renowned family therapist Virginia Satir, who helped thousands of families and individuals restore their emotional being within themselves and others.

With the permission of the V. Satir foundation, I developed this workbook with a goal in mind: to help children enhance their self esteem, and create more self awareness.

The poem, "My declaration of Self Esteem", is broken in sentences, so that the child understands each statement, and interacts in an activity that will help in creating self awareness.

I recommend its use with the company of an adult who can guide and create conversations related to the topics in the book, it is more effective to work on the book on leisure time, and without pressure to complete it.

I hope you enjoy the process and the bonding it will create in working with the child.

Sincerely,
Diana Malca Chern, LCSW
Registered Play Therapist Supervisor

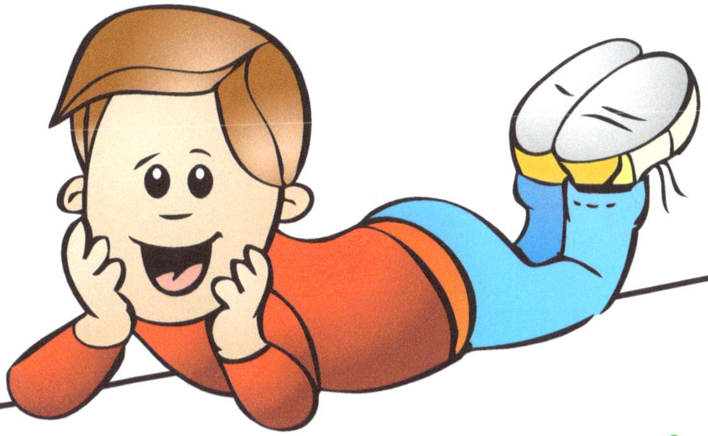

I am me

My Declaration of Self-Esteem
Based on Virginia Satir's Poem.

Illustrations by:
Francisco Ceron

From:

To:

I am me

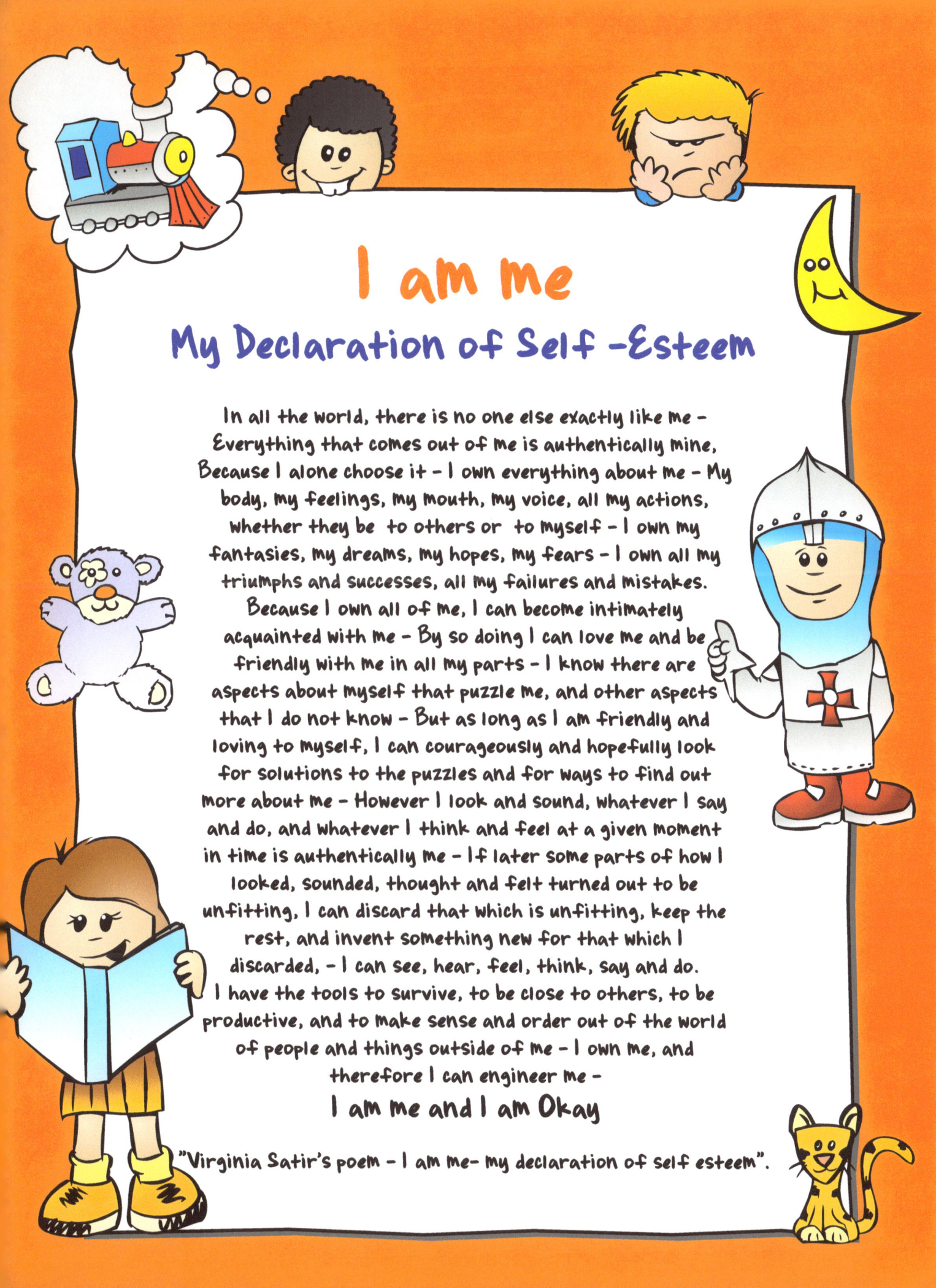

"There are people who have some parts like me, but no one adds up exactly like me"...

Who is like you?

Which traits are the same as yours?

Which traits are different than yours?

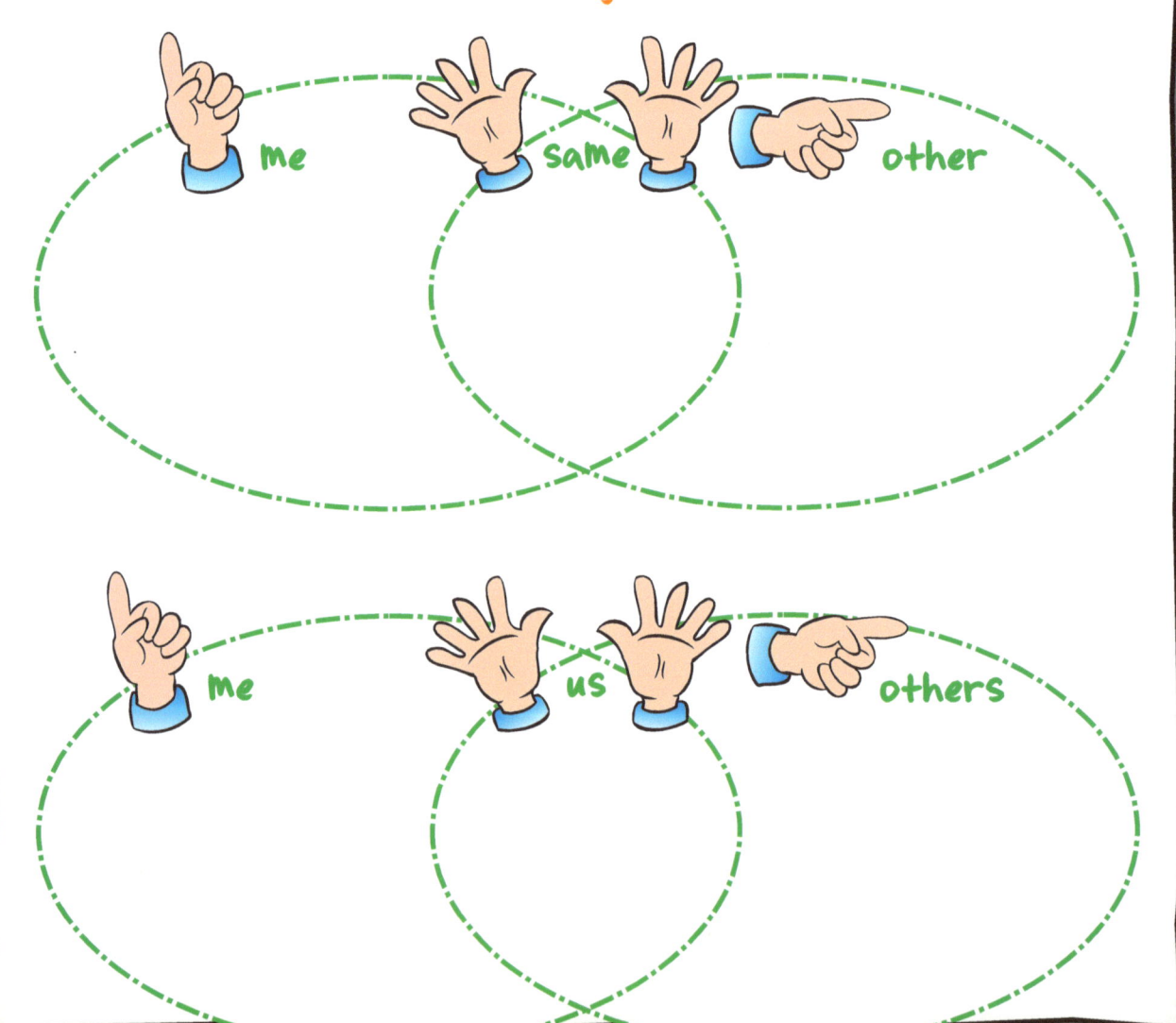

"My Mind: Including all its thoughts and ideas"...

What kind of thoughts do you have?

Encouraging?

Discouraging?

Positive? Negative?

What are your ideas?

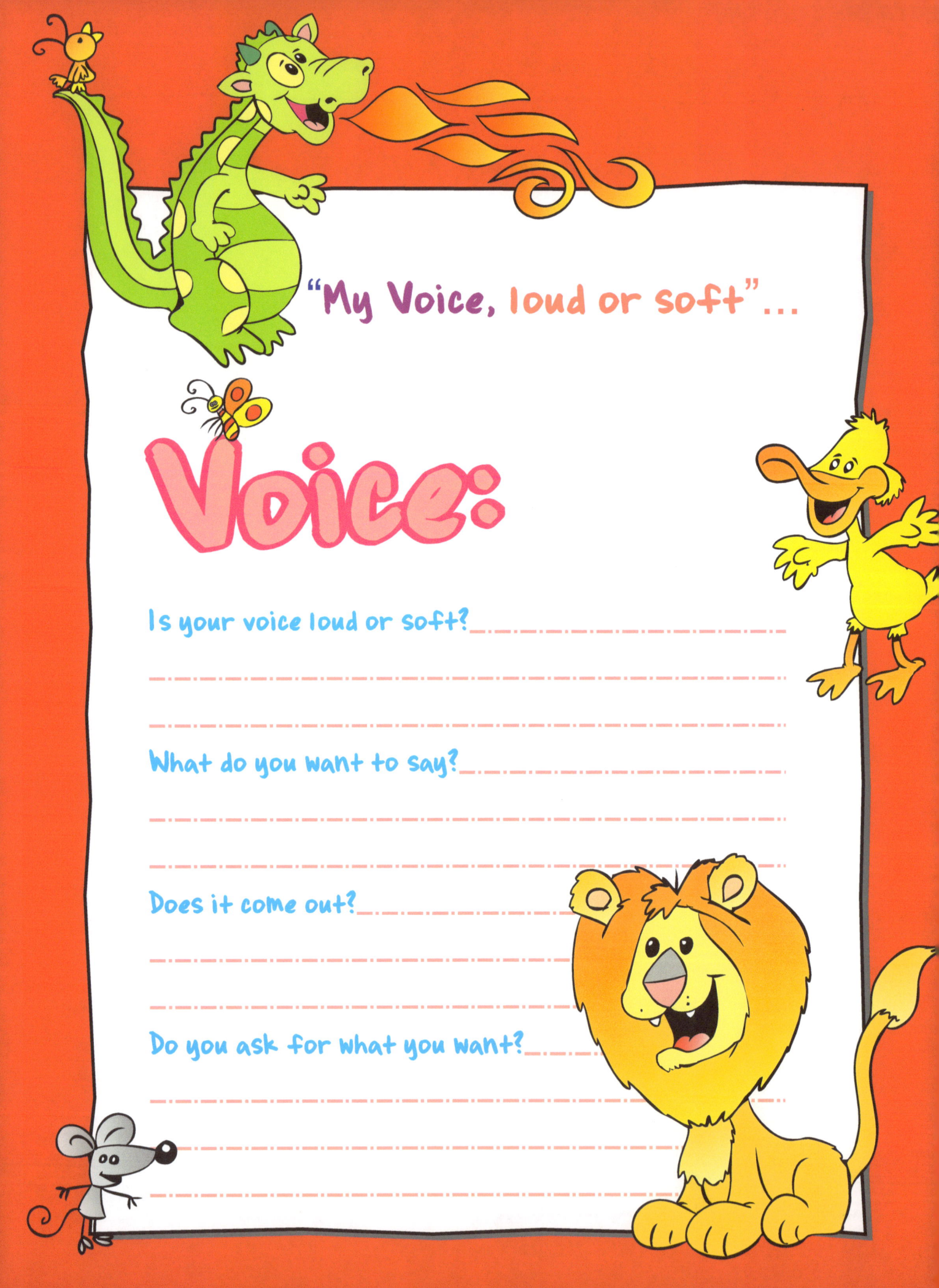

"My Voice, loud or soft"...

Voice:

Is your voice loud or soft? _____
_____
_____

What do you want to say? _____
_____
_____

Does it come out? _____
_____
_____

Do you ask for what you want? _____
_____
_____

"and all my actions whether they be to others or to myself"...

Do you act kindly? Aggressively? Friendly?

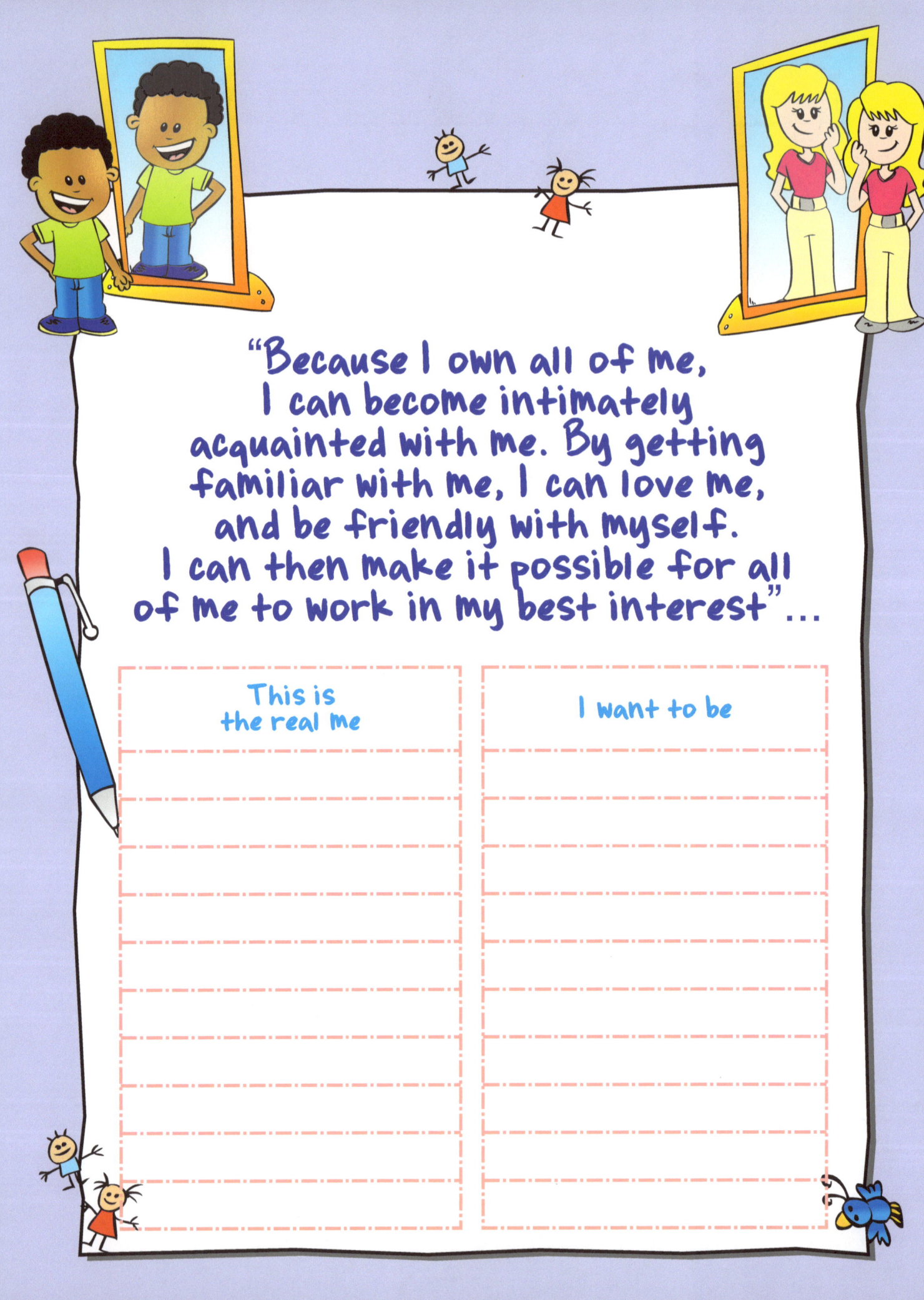

"Because I own all of me, I can become intimately acquainted with me. By getting familiar with me, I can love me, and be friendly with myself. I can then make it possible for all of me to work in my best interest"...

This is the real me	I want to be

"I know that there are aspects of myself that puzzle me, and other aspects that I do not know, but as long as I am friendly and loving to myself, I can courageously and hopefully look for the solutions to the puzzles and for ways to find out more"...

Make a puzzle of yourself:
In each piece draw things that describe a part of you!

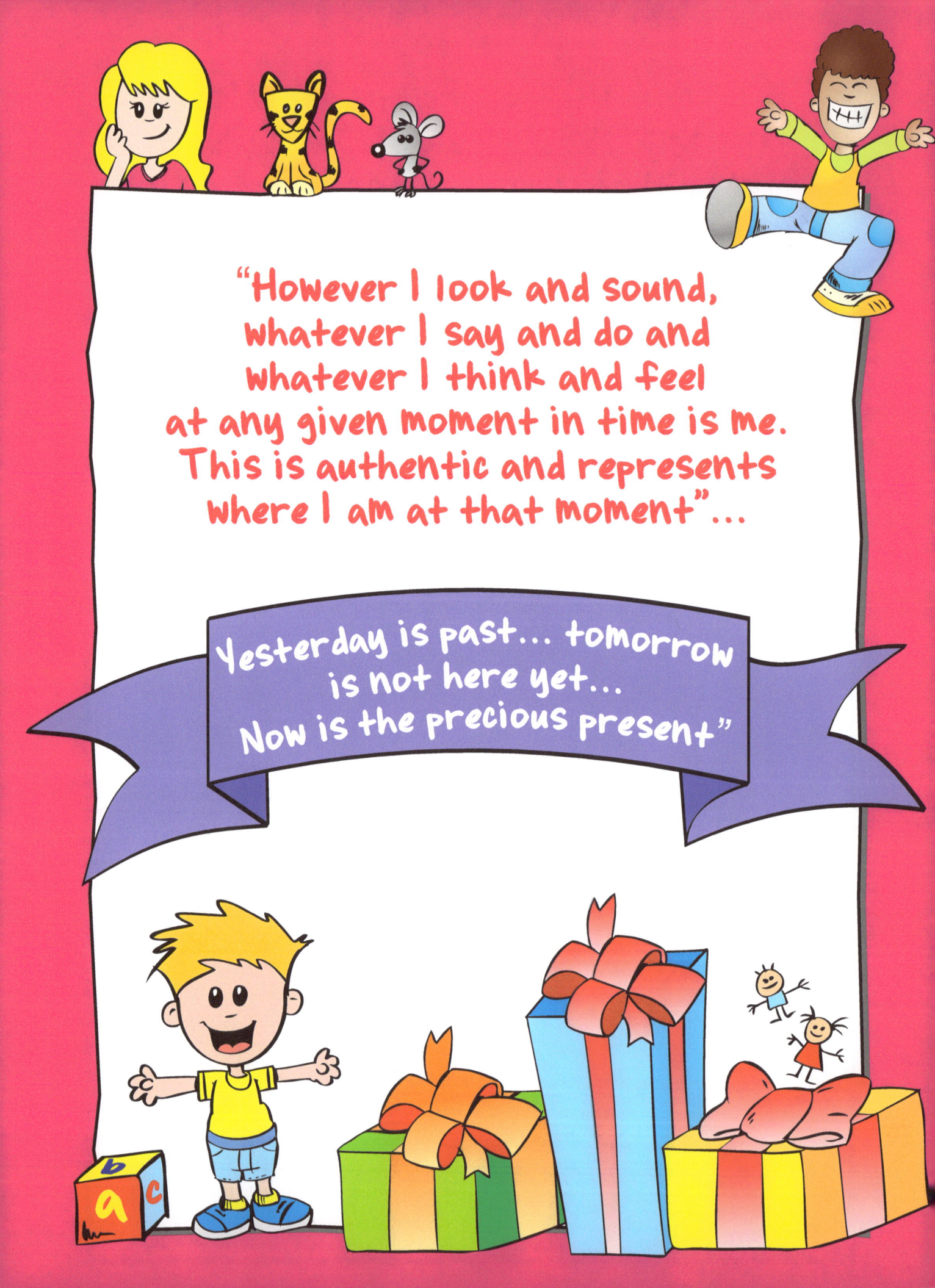

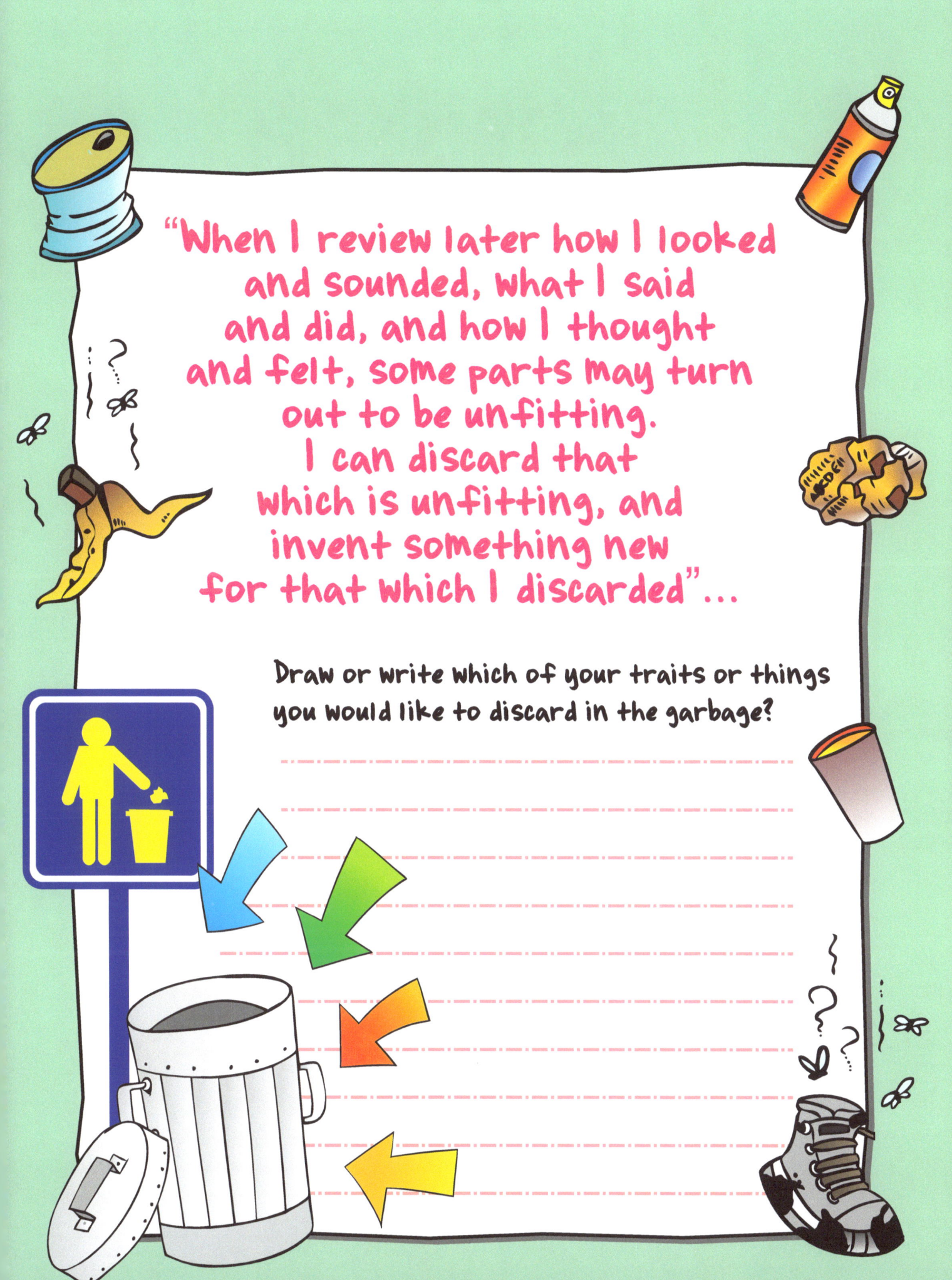

"When I review later how I looked and sounded, what I said and did, and how I thought and felt, some parts may turn out to be unfitting. I can discard that which is unfitting, and invent something new for that which I discarded"...

Draw or write which of your traits or things you would like to discard in the garbage?

"I can see, feel, think, say and do. I have the tools to survive, to be close to others, to be productive, and to make sense and order of the world of people and things outside of me"…

Word search:

```
B S E E T A L K O M E E
R E T H I N K O T Y V !
E N L A U G H V H S I D
A S A Y D O A E E E V L
T E C R E A T E R L R O
H C A R I N G S S F U V
E W O R L D E R A S S E
A X W L L D I N V E N T
```

See, sense, think, say, talk, invent, love, laugh, do, create, breathe, others, caring, myself, survive, world!

Copyright © 2012 Diana Malca Chern
All rights reserved.
ISBN:
ISBN-13: 978-0615602165
www.dianamalcachern.com

"1st edition. Printed in the USA"
"Copyright Healing Through Play, Corp. 2010"
"All rights reserved. no part of this workbook may be reproduced in any form or by any means electronic or mechanical, including photocopying, recording or by any information storage and retrieval system, without permission in writing from the publisher.

www.ingramcontent.com/pod-product-compliance
Lightning Source LLC
Chambersburg PA
CBHW042005150426
43194CB00002B/130